Old Inverkeithing
Edward Robinson

The time that Inverkeithing was one of Scotland's most important towns has long past. Now its major functions are as a dormitory for Edinburgh and as a commuter transportation hub. Inverkeithing Railway Station was built in 1890 and renovated in 1986. It is a very busy station because it is the last stop before the Fife Circle Line splits. As a result of its location, Inverkeithing receives more train services than any other place in Fife with ridership annually of one million passengers.

© Edward Robinson, 2012
First published in the United Kingdom, 2012,
by Stenlake Publishing Ltd
www.stenlake.co.uk
ISBN 9781840335996

The publishers regret that they cannot supply
copies of any pictures featured in this book.

This book is dedicated to the memory of David King (1937-2010), pictured right, an icon of Inverkeithing. He was the unofficial ambassador of the town and was known as "Mr. Inverkeithing" and "King of Inverkeithing". With his passing, his family received condolences from around the globe, Australia to America. He was a jolly man, full of fun, and a good friend. David also loved his home town with a deep passion and had a sweeping influence on Inverkeithing. One friend commented, "If it had not been for David, half of the stuff that Inverkeithing has would not be here." He was very active in promoting community activities including youth athletic clubs.

Aside from his family of wife Barbara, three sons (Calum, Murdo, and Gregor), and daughter (Tracey), his keenest interest was the history of his beloved Inverkeithing. He did a tremendous amount of research and published countless pamphlets regarding a wide spectrum of local history topics. In addition, he gave lectures regarding various aspects of Inverkeithing's history. His colleagues and friends were amazed at the breadth and depth of this remarkable man's knowledge of local history subjects. If anyone had a question regarding Inverkeithing, the standard answer would be "Ask David King". Considerable information gleaned from his booklets as well as many photographs from his collection are contained in this book.

Inverkeithing dedicated a bench in the Friary Gardens in memory of David. It was a very special place for the King family. His children recall him taking them to the gardens to play over 35 years ago.

The author, an American, is a descendant
of the Hendersons of Fordell.

INTRODUCTION

The Fife town of Inverkeithing sits beautifully on a terrace overlooking Inverkeithing Bay, an inlet of the Firth of Forth. Inverkeithing means "mouth of keithing", a small burn in the town. Over the years, the spelling of the town has varied considerably. It has been known as "Enderkeyden", "Henderkeyden", "Enderkeithing", "Invirkedin", "Inuirkeithin" and "Innerkeithing".

Every weekday thousands of people bypass Inverkeithing or zip through it on the Fife Circle Line without realising the past significance of the burgh. Located four miles southeast of Dunfermline, Inverkeithing was one of Scotland's most important royal burghs between the twelfth and sixteenth centuries.

The first written reference to Inverkeithing is in a foundation charter of Scone Abbey granted by Alexander I in 1114, but it is probably much older. Local tradition maintains that the Roman governor, Agricola, established a camp at the site circa 80 although documentation validating this assertion is lacking. The only early Roman evidence linking Rome with Inverkeithing was the discovery of a coin in the vicinity that was minted during the reign of Emperor Elagabalas (AD 218-222). Another key event in the early history of the burgh was the establishment of a chapel by St. Erat. Some historians place the date of St. Erat's Church circa 400 while others favour a date of circa 700 (hereafter the date of circa 400 will be used.) An early artefact found close to Inverkeithing is the so-called "Danish Stone" which dates to the 10th century or earlier.

Inverkeithing as a royal burgh is unusual in several ways. Firstly, it was among a few royal burghs that did not have a castle in the town or in the immediate vicinity. Secondly, the high streets of royal burghs tended to be rather narrow. Along with Crail, Inverkeithing had a broad high street. Thirdly, it was one of a few royal burghs that had a stone wall surrounding it. Other burghs that had stone walls included the wealthy towns of Edinburgh, Stirling, Perth, Dundee, Peebles, and Crail. During the medieval period, most of the houses in royal burghs were one storey. In sharp contrast, Inverkeithing had many two storey structures, several three storey residences, and even a four storey dwelling (the Galla Tower). Fourthly, relative to other royal burghs, Inverkeithing has a high portion of existing buildings that pre-date 1800.

Today Inverkeithing is a treasure trove of antiquities. Among its gems are a 14th century baptismal font in St. Peter's Parish Church which is regarded as the most beautiful medieval surviving church furnishing in Scotland, a mercat cross which is considered the most handsome among the oldest existing crosses in Scotland, a friary regarded as the best preserved friary in Scotland, and the stained glass window in St. Peter's Parish Church which was among the first installed in a Church of Scotland.

Inverkeithing was among the first Scottish royal burghs. William the Lion (ruled 1165-1214) confirmed the initial charter in about 1169. In addition, he granted Inverkeithing one of the more extensive hinterlands in Scotland. At one time, such towns as Culross, Kinross, Kinghorn, Dysart, and North Queensberry were subject to Inverkeithing's taxes and levies. Adding to the community's

The most important Scottish burghs were royal burghs that received charters from monarchs. These charters conveyed certain rights and privileges such as the authority to hold fairs and market days. In addition, royal burghs had a seat in the Scottish Parliament and were granted the right to trade with foreign countries. For many years, Inverkeithing was one of Scotland's leading seaports and a major contributor to the royal coffers. Inverkeithing was one of the first royal burghs, but the exact date of this status is unknown, although many historians believe it became a royal burgh during the 1153-1159 period. Royal burghs had a coat of arms and a town seal. Inverkeithing's coat of arms is divided into two parts. The left side shows a ship which represents the fact that this was once a prominent port. The right side shows St. Peter, the patron saint of the burgh, holding a model of the parish church and keys. The town seal displays a ship.

prestige royalty had residences here. David I had a house in town and Queen Annabella, consort of Robert III, sometimes lived here in the former friary. Moreover, several members of Scotland's aristocracy such as the Earl of Rosebery, the Earl of Morton, the Earl of Lauderdale, the Earl of Dunfermline, the Earl of Dunbar, and the Hendersons of Fordell had residences in Inverkeithing. Due to its significance, Inverkeithing has been mentioned in several literary works including Sorley MacLean's poem *The Clan*, Robert Louis Stevenson's novel *Kidnapped*, and Sir Walter Scott's novel *Old Mortality*. During its long history, Inverkeithing has served numerous and diverse functions, some concurrently. David I named it the ferry of Dunfermline and it was an important port for the shipment of wool and later of coal. For a considerable period, Inverkeithing conducted extensive sea trade with England and the Continent. It was also a fishing port, although this activity never reached the level of prominence that several other Fife ports attained.

Inverkeithing was a market town of considerable significance. As a royal burgh, it hosted weekly markets and at one time it held five annual fairs. King James IV bought his horses at Inverkeithing festivals and purchased two horses at a 1503 Inverkeithing Fair and four horses at a 1508 fair.

Although Inverkeithing was only a few miles from the great ecclesiastical town of Dunfermline, it was a religious focal point of substantial note. It is the site of one of the oldest churches in Scotland, St. Peter's. Two Catholic orders, the Franciscans and the Dominicans, constructed monasteries in Inverkeithing and in the 1100s a chapel was established. Reportedly, the Inverkeithing residences of David I and Queen Annabella had private chapels.

Inverkeithing was also a legislative centre. James II designated Inverkeithing in 1487 as the meeting site of the Convention of Royal Burghs. Later this honour was transferred to Edinburgh. On at least two occasions (1354 and 1423), councils of Parliament met in Inverkeithing.

Throughout much of its long history, Inverkeithing has been an industrial settlement. It had a carving horns and bones industry in the 1100s and the town had guilds by circa 1200. Ultimately, Inverkeithing had five guilds—hammermen, weavers, bakers, tailors, and shoemakers. Other commercial activities include brewing, brick making, distilling, ferrying, fishing, paper milling, pottery, quarrying, rope making, sail making, salt panning, shipbuilding, shipbreaking, tanning, and weaving.

The glory days of Inverkeithing are long gone. Fortunately there are a number of historic buildings and artefacts that still exist and harken back to the burgh's golden times. Historic Scotland classifies historic structures in three groups. Category A includes buildings of national and/or international importance. Category B covers buildings of regional significance while Category C applies to buildings of local prominence.

Inverkeithing has a number of A listings within the confines of the medieval burgh. These include the friary (circa 1350), the mercat cross (circa 1398), the Thomsoun House (1617), Fordell's Lodging (circa 1666), and the tolbooth (1754-1755). There are several noteworthy B listings as well. These include St. Peter's Parish Church (with a 14th century tower), Rosebery House (late 1500s), Providence House (circa 1688), Inverkeithing Railway Station, and Inverkeithing Harbour.

Other A listings near Inverkeithing include Fordell Castle, Fordell Castle Chapel, Forth Bridge, and St. Bridget's Kirk.

ACKNOWLEDGEMENTS

Many people provided invaluable assistance in the preparation of this book. I am deeply indebted to the family of David King for their extensive inputs. Without the help of my friend, historian, and educator, Kim Traynor, this book would not have been completed. I would like to thank Harry Sprange, President of the Inverkeithing Local History Society, for his important assistance as well as other members of the Society for their help. In addition, I appreciate the aid of Neil Fraser of the Royal Commission of Ancient and Historic Monuments of Scotland and Daphne McFarlane and her staff at the Inverkeithing Library. Most of all, I would like to acknowledge the support and encouragement of my wife, Susan, and my aunt, Helen Watson. Stenlake's talented staff was extremely helpful in various aspects of producing this book.

A concerted effort was made to acknowledge the organisations whose photographs were used in this book. Any omissions in this regard were unintentional and regretted by the author.

The publishers are unable supply copies of any pictures in this book.

INVERKEITHING AND ENVIRONS HISTORY TIMELINE

*c.*400. St. Erat founds a wooden church at Inverkeithing.

1100s. A Norman church built on the site of St. Erat's.

1120. Inverkeithing listed as the only trading community in Fife.

1120. An old document lists Inverkeithing containing a church, a royal palace, and a few houses. The population was estimated as being between 100 and 150.

*c.*1126. St. Peter's Church gifted to Dunfermline Abbey.

*c.*1129. David I grants the monks and abbots of Dunfermline the passage of the ship of Inverkeithing.

1165. Merchant guilds at Inverkeithing were established.

1178. St. Bridget's Church in Dalgety constructed by this date.

1196. Hospital built in Inverkeithing.

1244. St. Peter's church dedicated by Bishop David de Bernham on the site of St. Erat's Church and a later Norman church.

1250. Local tradition maintains that groups favoring the Culdee form of worship and the Roman style of worship met at St. Peter's Church to resolve their religious conflicts. The decision was that the Culdees were in the wrong. This assemblage of Culdees was among the last in Scotland.

1268. The Franciscan Order established in Inverkeithing.

1286. Inverkeithing is the last place King Alexander III was seen alive before his fatal fall from a horse near Kinghorn.

1296. Inverkeithing's coat of arms and town seal were in use.

1327. Inverkeithing ranked seventh among Scottish sea ports in terms of custom receipts.

*c.*1350. Franciscans built Greyfriars Monastery (the only remaining structure is the hospitium). This building has been known as "The Palace", "Rothmills Inn", and "The Inns".

*c.*1375. King Robert III and his Queen Annabella Drummond give a baptismal font to St. Peter's Parish Church.

1379. Fire ravages Inverkeithing.

1398. Inverkeithing's mercat cross thought to have been erected at this time to commemorate the marriage of Robert III and Annabella's first son, the Duke of Rothesay, to Mary Douglas. Recent scholars tend to believe that the cross may have been erected at a later date, probably in the early 16th century.

*c.*1401. Queen Annabella, who sometimes resided at the former Friary, dies. She is buried at Dunfermline Abbey.

1423. A General Council meets in Inverkeithing and selects a group to meet with the regent of England to secure the release of the future James I. The ransom was 40,000 pounds.

1487. Inverkeithing hosts the Convention of Royal Burghs.

16th century. Although in medieval times Inverkeithing was often a wealthy burgh, the town council complained several times of its weak economic condition in this century. Eventually the town recovered, but never again reached its former power and glory.

1504. King James IV holds court in Inverkeithing.

1500s. The Scott House and the House of the Holburnes constructed on Church Street as well as the Rosebery House on King Street.

1596. The Hendersons of Fordell start mining coal less than two miles from Fordell Castle. For several years, the coal initially was taken by horse and pannier to Inverkeithing for shipment overseas.

1608-9. Epidemic of the plague in the burgh.

1612. Galla Tower erected on High Street.

1651. Battle of Inverkeithing. Oliver Cromwell's army decisively defeats the Scots Royalists. Much of the battle was in the vicinity of Pitreavie Castle—two miles from Inverkeithing. Several villages, including Inverkeithing, were burned and plundered by the Parliamentary Army.

1661. Mary, Queen of Scots visits Inverkeithing.

1720s. Noted author Daniel Defoe writes, {Inverkeithing} is large… but decayed. He was impressed by the town's bay and its bustling linen industry.

1721. The Hendersons construct Fordell House close to Fordell Castle.

1735. Samuel Grieg (d. 1789), Inverkeithing's most famous native son, was born at the Royal Hotel (now the Half Crown pub) on High Street. Grieg is known as the Father of the Russian Navy.

1752. St. John's Church, a burgher church, established.

1752. Sir John Henderson of Fordell creates a port at St. David's Bay (now part of the town of Dalgety Bay) for the shipment of coal.

1754. The tolbooth, a square tower building, constructed. The main block was erected in 1770.

1755. Post office opens in Inverkeithing.

*c.*1769. A wooden waggonway built from the Fordell coalfields to St. David's Bay.

*c.*1783. The Halbeath-Inverkeithing Old Wagon Road (eight miles long) established. Coal from the Halbeath and Townhill pits was carried by horse to Inverkeithing Harbour for shipment.

*c.*1806. St. Peter's Church's baptismal font found during church repairs. The grey sandstone font was found under the floor of the tower (apparently it had been concealed at the time of the Reformation). The bowl is decorated with angels holding heraldic shields.These include the Arms of Scotland as well as those of Queen Annabella Drummond. The carvings on the font represent exceptional workmanship.

1824. Among Scottish towns, Inverkeithing has the most consistent record for sending petitions against the slave trade and slavery.

1825. An accidental fire destroys much of St. Peter's Church, but the west tower and the font survived. Over the following two years, the church was rebuilt. The present church is a handsome building constructed in the Gothic style.

1827. A large distillery is established on Boreland Road.

1828. Cruicks Quarry opened.

1842. Queen Victoria and Prince Albert visit.

1843. Inverkeithing was an important seaport particularly for coal exports with 28 ships registered at the port.

1858-1888. Shipbuilding flourished.

1882. The forerunner of the Caldwell Paper Mill established.

1890. Forth Bridge dedicated.

1914. The Caldwell Paper Mill burned down, but it was quickly rebuilt.

1920s. Shipbreaking becomes the industry most associated with Inverkeithing in the 20th century.

1923. Inverkeithing war memorial dedicated. Originally erected on the site of Scott's House next to Fordell's Lodging, in 1973 it was moved to an attractive park across the street and next to St. Peter's Parish Church.

1937. Among the famous ships that met their end in Inverkeithing's Ward Shipbreaking Yards were the White Star ships, the *Olympic* and the *Homeric*.

1939. Forth Bridge survives an attack by German bombers.

1951. 300th anniversary celebration of the Battle of Inverkeithing was held at the mercat cross.

1963. Fordell House demolished.

1964. Forth Road Bridge completed.

1964. Scotland's first Enterprise Town of Dalgety Bay was established, encompassing the area where the small village of St. David's Bay once stood.

Early 1980s. Shipbreaking yard closes down.

1991. Inverkeithing Local History Society founded.

1994. A commemorative stained glass window highlighting the history of St. Peter's Church and the burgh of Inverkeithing is installed in the church.

2003. Caldwell Paper Mill ceases operations. Thousands of local residents had worked there.

2006. St. Peter's and St. John's churches merge into one congregation. St. Peter's Church underwent repairs and the congregation met at St. John's.

2008. The new Civic Center next to the Friary completed. The facility houses a library and several historical exhibits that once were displayed in the museum at the Friary.

2011. With repairs completed, St. Peter's Church is again the parish church. The congregations of St. Peter's and St. John's are reunited at St. Peter's for the first time in 259 years.

BIBLIOGRAPHY

Cunningham, Andrew S., *Inverkeithing, North Queensferry, Limekilns, Charlestown, the Ferry Hills*, 1899

Ewan, Elizabeth, *Townlife in Fourteenth-Century Scotland*, 1990

Fife Council, *Inverkeithing Conservation Area Appraisal and Management Plan, Draft* 2011

Gifford, John, *The Buildings of Scotland, Fife*, 1988

Inglis, J. C. and F. Inglis, *The Fordell Railway*, 1946

Lamont-Brown, Raymond, *Fife in History and Legend*, 2002

Mair, Craig, *Mercat Cross and Tolbooth*, 1988

Naismith, Robert J., *The Story of Scotland's Towns*, 1989

Omand, Donald (ed.), *The Fife Book*, 2000

Simpson, Anne Turner and Stevenson, Sylvia, *Historic Inverkeithing: The Archaeological Implication of Development*, 1981

Smith, Alexander, *The Third Statistical Account of Scotland, The County of Fife*, 1952

Stephen, William, *History of Inverkeithing and Rosyth*, 1921

Stephen, William, *The Story of Inverkeithing and Rosyth*, 1938

Wordsworth, Jonathan, *Excavations in Inverkeithing*, 1981

The map shows that the street pattern still retains its medieval design of one major street with wynds branching out from it. As the principal street progresses through the town from south to north its name changes from Hope Street to High Street to Church Street to Chapel Place. Many medieval royal burghs were quite small both in terms of area and population. Inverkeithing was no exception to this. The area encompassed by Inverkeithing's stone walls was less than half a square mile. The estimated population of Inverkeithing in 1700 was 1,630.

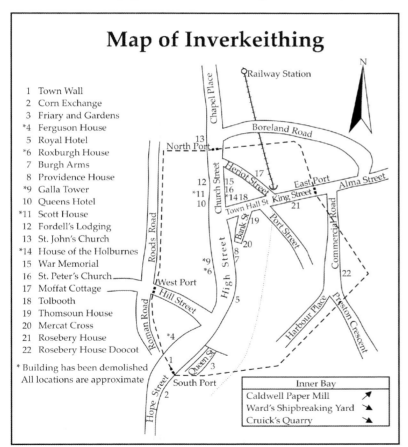

Map of Inverkeithing

1 Town Wall
2 Corn Exchange
3 Friary and Gardens
*4 Ferguson House
5 Royal Hotel
*6 Roxburgh House
7 Burgh Arms
8 Providence House
*9 Galla Tower
10 Queens Hotel
*11 Scott House
12 Fordell's Lodging
13 St. John's Church
*14 House of the Holburnes
15 War Memorial
16 St. Peter's Church
17 Moffat Cottage
18 Tolbooth
19 Thomsoun House
20 Mercat Cross
21 Rosebery House
22 Rosebery House Doocot

* Building has been demolished
All locations are approximate

Railway Station

Chapel Place
Boreland Road
North Port
Church Street
Heriot Street
East Port
Alma Street
King Street
Town Hall St
Roods Road
Bank St
Port Street
Commercial Road
High Street
West Port
Hill Street
Roman Road
Harbour Place
Preston Crescent
Queen St
Hope Street
South Port

Inner Bay	
Caldwell Paper Mill	↗
Ward's Shipbreaking Yard	↘
Cruick's Quarry	↘

In 1752, Inverkeithing tore down most of its walls. The photograph on the right below shows a portion of the town wall near the West Port and Roman Road.

The North Port was at Church Street while the East Port was on King Street. The South Port was at Hope Street and the West Port was located at Hill Street. After the ports were demolished, markers were placed at their former locations. The image left shows the only surviving one, the East Port marker. Its inscription reads Site of East Port 16th Century.

80068.

Although Hope Street – seen here looking north – is one of the major streets of Inverkeithing, it was outside the walls of the medieval burgh. South Port was to its north. Two of Inverkeithing's principal buildings during the medieval era are believed to have been situated on Hope Street. An 1196 document made reference to the hospital of Inverkeithing which historians believe was located at what is now 1-11 Hope Street. A mid-12th century document referred to a chapel at Inverkeithing and a later charter states that the chapel was outside of the town. The exact location of this building is unknown, but it may have been the old building situated at the rear of 8-14 Hope Street referred to as a chapel as late as the 1800s. Another structure on Hope Street that no longer exists was a milestone, located at the northern end of the street, which indicated that the distances to Kinross and North Queensferry were fourteen and two miles, respectively.

The photograph on the left shows Hope Street looking south. The large buildings on the right occupy 1-11 Hope Street, the possible medieval site of a hospital. Buildings at this address are directly across the street from the Old Corn Exchange.

This rather plain, but distinguished two storey neo-classical building is built of sandstone ashlar and is located at 2 Hope Street. It was constructed in 1833 (the front of the building has a date stone in roman numerals) as the Corn Exchange to handle the burgh's active commercial business. Originally the building was to have a belfry, but it was judged to be unstable and that project was dropped. By 1896 it ws serving as a drill hall for the town's pipe band and for many years it was commonly referred to as the Piper's Hall. Over the years the building has had a number of occupants including the Boy Scouts, plumbers, an ambulance garage, joiners, used car sales room, and a chemist's laboratory. Historic Scotland has classified the structure as a B listed historic building.

One of Inverkeithing's greatest prizes is the Franciscan friary located on Queen Street. It is an A listed building and generally regarded as the best preserved friary in Scotland. The Franciscans were established at Inverkeithing circa 1268 and the friary was constructed circa 1350. The friary was a busy place in the 1300s, hosting pilgrims from the south headed to the religious shrines at St. Andrews and Dunfermline. Around 1400, Queen Annabella Drummond, wife of Robert III and mother of James I, used the friary as one of her residences, hence why Queen Street is so-named. With the storm clouds of the Reformation looming, ownership of the friary in 1559 was transferred from the Catholic church to a secular owner, John Swynton, a burgess of Inverkeithing, in an attempt to save the friary from destruction. Unfortunately, the only building to survive was the hospitium located on the west range of the friary. Although the friary underwent renovations in the 17th century, it still retains much of its 14th century character. In the mid-1930s, it was renovated again. This photograph shows the front of the friary (the building with the forestairs) after several of its 20th century refinements. All of the other buildings on this side of the street have been demolished. Their removal facilitated access to the Friary Gardens. (Photo courtesy of the Royal Commission on the Ancient and Historic Monuments of Scotland hereafter referred to as RCAHMS.)

This 1860s photograph focuses on the back of the friary (the east elevation). On the north elevation gable, there is evidence of previously attached buildings. Other than the hospitium, the only other surviving structures are some ruined vaulted cellars and two wells. To the rear are some lovely gardens, of which only a small portion is visible here and out of shot is a playground that was constructed in the mid-1930s and nearby the location of an orchard during medieval times. In the latter part of the 20th century and early part of 21st century, the hospitium housed the Inverkeithing Museum. The building's first floor serves as a senior citizen centre with the second floor used for storage. (Photo courtesy of the Inverkeithing Local History Society hereafter referred to as ILHS.)

For centuries, the hub of commercial activity has been High Street. In 1862 there were some 30 businesses representing 12 different trades on the street, ranging from grocers to china merchants. One of the older residences was the Ferguson House that formerly occupied 97-99 High Street. The building had two pediments bearing the date 1679 and the initials R. F. and B. D. which stood for Robert Ferguson and his wife, Beatrice Douglas. Ferguson, a bailie of Inverkeithing, passed away in 1684. Two of the most interesting later owners were Mary and Agnes Berry who acquired the house in 1817. The sisters were members of an elite London social set. Mary was an accomplished author. Both sisters died in 1852.

The three storey building located at 36-38-40 High Street was built during the 1670-1680 period and has a sharply pitched roof and narrow windows, features typical of 17th century buildings. Adjoining this building is a three storey 18th century structure once known as the Royal Hotel and now the Half Crown pub. Florence Grieg, a shipowner and a burgess acquired the property in 1719. Ownership then passed to his son, Charles, who was also a shipowner. Charles was the father of Samuel (1735-1788), Inverkeithing's most famous son who would become known as *The Father of the Russian Navy*. In 1763, the Court of Catherine the Great requested the loan of British officers to help upgrade and modernise the Russian Navy. Samuel's superior abilities soon became evident and ultimately he earned the rank of grand admiral. He distinguished himself both at sea and on land being the hero of the 1770 Battle of Chesma against the Turks and the 1788 Battle of Hogland versus Swedes. He improved Russia's naval defences, enhanced their code of discipline, and instilled a strong sense of pride among members of the fleet. Over the years, Empress Catherine bestowed him with many honours including an estate in Livonia, the governorship of Kronstadt, and a knighthood. When Samuel contracted a fever and died, the empress ordered a state funeral in his honour and a statue honouring Samuel was erected in the city of Tallinn.

While it seems improbable that a Scotsman would be named an admiral of the Russian Imperial Navy, there were in fact two that attained this honour in the 18th century. Incredibly, William Roxburgh (circa1735 – circa1785) was also from the small town of Inverkeithing. He and Samuel Grieg were among the first five officers selected to serve in the Russian Navy in 1763. Cousins, they were raised on the same street. Roxburgh was a skillful mariner and was promoted in 1766 to captain of the first rank. In 1773, he advanced to commodore and received the honour of knighthood of St. George. Roxburgh was promoted to rear admiral in 1776 and later that year he retired from service ending his distinguished career. William was the son of William Roxburgh, merchant, bailie and Dean of the Guild of Inverkeithing. The younger William grew up at 11-15 High Street, a two storey tenement with two external staircases. The Roxburgh family acquired the east part of the tenement in 1641 and the west part in 1705. The property stayed with the Roxburghs, frequently a family of shipowners, to the late 19th century. As the photo shows, the first floor was used as a cycle shop in the early 20th century. The structure was demolished in 1921.

At 16-20-22 High Street, there is an inset triangular pediment bearing the dates of 1664 and 1888. Alexander Anderson constructed the earlier structure, a townhouse, and it was known as the Anderson House. Reportedly this building was among the finest in Inverkeithing. At least two well-known people spent time here—James Boswell (1740-1795), the biographer of Dr. Samuel Johnson, and the Presbyterian minister, John Blackadder (1622-1685). The Burgh Arms Hotel was built in 1888 on the site of the Anderson House.

One of Inverkeithing's most distinctive buildings is the three storey Providence House located on the north side of the Burgh Arms Hotel at 12-14-18 High Street. The building, a B listed historical structure, derives its name from an inscribed lintel. Above the moulded doorway are the initials *I. B.* and the date *1688*. The inscription reads *God's Providence Is My Inheritance*. The initials stand for Isobel Bairlie. She and her first husband, Alexander Anderson, a merchant, burgess, and builder, purchased the house in 1687 from James Kinglassie. Alexander, who built the 1664 structure next door, passed away in 1687. Isobel erected the addition after receiving permission from the town council to extend the west wall into the street nine feet beyond the original line of the frontage. The 1688 date refers to this addition and not the main block which was built before the property transfer. Other former owners of the building include a provost, a town clerk, and a bookbinder. Over the years, a number of business concerns have been located on the first floor including a restaurant, a travel agency, and an optometrist's office.

Near the northwest end of High Street stood a massive tenement of unique design known as the Galla Tower which had a four storey tower that adjoined a three storey main block. The building was harled and had a pantiled roof. Inside the structure were two inscribed stones. One read *God Bless Harie Kinglassie and Bessie Brown Their Posterity and All of Their Friends*. The other stone bore the date *1612*. Harie was a town councillor. Circa 1704, the first Earl of Rosebery acquired the structure, selling it in 1721. Other owners included a bookbinder and two physicians. The building was demolished in 1890 to make room for the Clydesdale Bank building. (Photo courtesy of ILHS.)

This photograph shows the north end of High Street which was the location of the medieval market place (confirmed by an archaeological excavation in 1981) and the annual fairs. Identifiable buildings in the photo include the Royal Hotel on the near right. The structure in the centre of the picture is an early 18th century two storey townhouse that has been converted to a restaurant on the first floor with a flat above. Behind this structure are two buildings that are on Church Street. The first is the House of Holburnes of Menstrie, now demolished. To its north is the 14th century tower of St. Peter's Parish Church. To the right of the 19th century building is the Providence House, the tall white structure. To the south of Providence House stands the Burgh Arms Hotel.

Inverkeithing held four fairs per year as early as 1640 and a fifth fair was added in 1695. These festivals were in March, May, June, August, and October. Dunfermline burgh records show that sessions were postponed because it was fair day at Inverkeithing. All five fairs existed until 1836. Now only the Lammas Fair in August is active. Originally the fairs focused on the trade of livestock (cattle, sheep, and horses) and the sale of products such as dairy and bakery goods, clothing, shoes, linen, and wool. As time progressed, entertainment became a principal aspect and the market features declined in importance. Inverkeithing's burgh records of 1652 have this entry… *it was a great day for fun, frolic, fit races, ale, and drunken folks, gentle, and folks cam frae near and far to it.*

The photograph above shows a crowd watching as children enjoy an exciting ride. The Lammas Fair started with the much-loved hat and ribbon race which is a centuries old tradition. Originally the race was held for shepherd lads. The winner won the hat and the ribbon was for his lady fair. The race is still conducted with considerable ritual preceded by a procession led by the town council with a representative bearing a hat and ribbon on a halberd. Multiple races are now held for boys and girls of different age groups and the prizes are trophies. To be chosen queen of the fair was a great honour. The picture top right shows Miss M. R. Houliston crowning Sybil Hunter as the 1937 queen. The king was Kenneth Grindley. The pages included James Temple, Collin Phillips, Harry Gray, and Robert Portieous.

An important date in the history of Inverkeithing was 6th September 1842. On that day Queen Victoria and Prince Albert visited the burgh with an estimated 15,000 people in attendance. This assemblage was the largest in the history of Inverkeithing as people came from a wide area to greet the monarch. This was the first visit to Inverkeithing by a ruler since Charles II. A cannon blast announced the arrival of the royal party at the West Port. An imposing triumphal arch was erected there which was crowned by evergreens and flags. The church, the steeple, many homes, and buildings were decorated with buntings and flags to celebrate the memorable occasion. A platform was erected on High Street and a loyal and patriotic address was presented to the queen and her consort.

Church Street, one of the most important streets in Inverkeithing, is an extension of High Street to the north. Located here is St. Peter's Parish Church, the war memorial, the Queens Hotel, and Fordell's Lodging. In the past, two 16th century houses, two 17th century houses, and two schools were sited on the street. The Queens Hotel (left) is a late 19th century two storey structure which until the early 1900s was a posting hotel with horses and carriages for rent. In 2010 it was converted from a hotel to an apartment building. Its High Victorian style is striking. After this photograph was taken, the colour scheme was changed to a distinctive black and white pattern.

The 1890 image (on the right) shows to the left the stables of the Queens Hotel, the Scott House (the house with the forestairs), and Fordell's Lodging (the building with the turret). The Scott House, built of stone, consisted of two blocks. The newer one next to Fordell's Lodging was added in 1621. Scottish houses of stone were not common until the 17th century. Some historians estimate that the original portion of the Scott House dates to the 16th century or possibly earlier. A 16th century owner of the house was Andrew Scott, a burgess of Inverkeithing, who lived here until his death in 1589. The building was sometimes referred to as the Burgess House. Some historians believe that James IV spent a night here. Early owners included three generations of the Hendersons of Fordell, surgeon John Dungas, and schoolmaster James Melrose. The Scott House was demolished in 1913 to improve access to a new school built across the street.

Fordell's Lodging, a Category A building, is located at 16-18 Church Street across the street from St. Peter's Parish Church. It was built for Sir John Henderson of Fordell circa 1666. His principal residence was at Fordell Castle which was located nearby. The design of the three storey Church Street building with its two-stage turret resembles the castle to a considerable extent. The building has a steeply pitched roof and crow-stepped gables. Fordell's Lodging served as a prototype for the Scottish Baronial architecture that became popular in the 19th century. On the north interior wall is a carved representation of the coat of arms of Charles II. Mary, Queen of Scots named the Hendersons hereditary provosts of Inverkeithing. As was the case with the Scott's House, three generations of Hendersons owned Fordell's Lodging. Interestingly, two other owners of the Scott House, Dr. John Dungas and James Melrose, were also owners of Fordell's Lodging. The parish minister Alan Buchanan bought the Fordell's Lodging in 1747. For a time, the burgh's post office was housed in the basement. The Episcopal Church of Inverkeithing met here briefly in the early 1900s. St. Peter's Parish Church acquired the building in 1907. From the 1920s until 2009, Fordell's Lodging served as the church hall of St. Peter's Church. In 2009, a private individual purchased the property.

The B listed St. John's Church is located on Chapel Place. St. John's has had an interesting history, with some of the congregation splitting off from the mother church over a controversy regarding the appointment of a minister in 1752. The first minister of the new church fell out of favour with the majority of the congregation near the end of his ministry. At least once, one of the preacher's strong supporters allegedly stood holding a gun while the minister delivered his sermon. Ultimately, this minister was suspended. The second minister also had difficulty with the congregation and he too was suspended. With the selection of their third minister (22-year Ebenezer Brown) in 1780, St. John's Church was more fortunate. During his tenure spanning 56 years the church thrived and flourished. Rev. Brown was noted for his piety and saintly demeanor. Many of his parishioners regarded him as the greatest speaker they had ever heard. His reputation spread throughout Scotland. Churches at Stirling, Aberdeen, and Glasgow all attempted to lure him away from his post in Inverkeithing. Their efforts were to no avail as Rev. Brown steadfastly stayed at Inverkeithing.

This photograph shows St. Peter's Parish Church and to the south the House of the Holburnes of Menstrie. The tolbooth located at the extreme right of the image is on Townhall Street. The building between the Holburne House and the tolbooth housed a grocery. This picture illustrates how compact much of medieval Inverkeithing was. An early resident of the Holburne House was Sir Adam Angill, a schoolmaster. In 1591, Thomas Mitchell, a burgess of Inverkeithing, acquired the property. William Inglis of Otterson purchased the house in 1629. The building ultimately passed to Inglis' daughter Elizabeth, the wife of Major-General Holburne of Menstrie. The couple married in 1648 at St. Peter's Parish Church. The house stayed in the Holburne family until the early 1700s. At that time, John Cant, town clerk and his wife Jean Mowbray, purchased it. They sold it in 1718.

Although St. Peter's Parish Church, located appropriately on Church Street is only a B listed building, few churches in Fife are more historic. St. Erat erected a small church here in the 400s. St. Erat's Holy Well is located underneath Heriot Street between Moffat Cottage and St. Peter's Parish Church. The original church was replaced by a Norman structure in the early 12th century. The foundations of the Norman church were incorporated into a Gothic church constructed in the early 1200s. This structure was consecrated by Bishop David de Bernham in 1244 and dedicated to St. Peter. Local tradition maintains that this church in 1250 was the final assemblage of the Culdees in Scotland as they were overpowered by those favouring the Romish style of worship. The buttressed four-stage west tower was added in the 1300s. An 1825 fire destroyed most of the church other than the west tower and the font. The church was rebuilt in 1826-27. In 1900, the church underwent extensive interior repairs and renovations resulting in a more inviting church with an airy and spacious appearance. The present church is a combination of three buildings. A few stones from the Norman church are retained in the lower walls toward the rear of the church and the walls of the choir and the tower remain from the Gothic church as well as the baptismal font, but the majority of the church is a 19th century structure.

The spire built in 1852 replaced one constructed in 1731 and one of the first stained glass windows in a Church of Scotland structure was installed in 1856-7. The clock was gifted by Mr. J.T. Smith in 1883. It was originally intended to grace the tolbooth tower, but when Smith realised that he could not see the clock from his residence, it was shifted to the church. Among the treasures of the church is the bell in the belfry cast in The Netherlands in 1641, two silver cups (1643), bronze alms dishes from Nuremburg, Germany (circa 1650), communion tokens dating back to 1674, two pewter flagons and cups (1705), a pewter plate (1765), and two communion cups (1821). Gravestones (the earliest one is dated 1606) surround three sides of the church.

St. Peter's Church baptismal font (left) is generally regarded as Scotland's finest surviving medieval church furnishing. The vast majority of Scottish medieval fonts are simple and circular in shape and have little ornamental carved work. In sharp contrast, the Inverkeithing font, made of grey sandstone, is hexagonal in shape and complex in design. The carving is exquisite. The coat of arms of Robert III and his queen, Annabella, are displayed. It is believed that the couple presented the font to St. Peter's on the occasion of the baptism of their son David, the Duke of Rothesay, in 1375.

Each of six sides of the font has a large shield supported by an angel with wings extended. The lower part of the font consists of five short filleted shafts. The shafts stand on projected bases standing on an octagonal plinth. The font stands four feet and one inch high. The bowl is three feet and two inches across.

That the font now occupies a place in the church close to the pulpit is due to a stroke of good fortune. Around 1806 when workmen were repairing the church they found the bowl of the font wrapped in straw beneath the floor of the tower where it had been hidden for safe keeping just prior to the Scottish Reformation. For many years, the base of the font had been ignored as it lay in the churchyard, its function not evident.

In 1994, St. Peter's received a striking addition, a stained glass window commemorating the 750th anniversary of the dedication of the church. This stained glass window graphically illustrates the close connection between the history of St. Peter's Parish Church and that of Inverkeithing. At first, the window with its detail may be hard to interpret. Upon closer examination, however, the rich history of the church and of the town unfolds. The window is ablaze with vivid colors dominated by purple, aqua, pink, and orange hues. Starting at the top and descending through the window are the six heraldic shields each carried by an angel. Near the top is St. Erat's Church with a straw roof. Just below is St. Erat, with Bible in hand, preaching to the congregation in front of the Holy Well.

High up on the right side is Moby the whale. Moby was stranded in the Forth about the time that the window was being designed. Further down is a scene of the 1825 fire that destroyed much of the Gothic church. Continuing downward is the present church restored with an angel on the roof.

The Caldwell Paper Mill which employed many residents of Inverkeithing through the years is represented by circles depicting rolls of paper. The Forth Bridge has a noticeable position and the towers of the Forth Road Bridge are also displayed. Under the bridges is a net of fish characterizing St. Peter as well as life along the Forth River.

Agricultural life is embodied by a farmer and a horse-drawn cart. Below the cart is a quarry on a hill which honours an industry that has been important to the residents of Inverkeithing. The font characterizes the sacramental life of the church. The mercat cross on the lower left side represents a secular aspect of community life.

OLD GRAMMAR SCHOOL AND PARISH CHURCH, INVERKEITHING. 23088.JV.

The Old Grammar School was located on the north side of St. Peter's Parish Church. The distinctive building, which featured an impressive belfry, was built in 1820. It was demolished in 1972 to make room for the war memorial, formerly located across the street on the site previously occupied by the Scott House, next to the south side of Fordell's Lodging.

In 1229, a lodging house for the monks of Arbroath Abbey was constructed on the future site of Moffat Cottage. The church maintained the property until the Scottish Reformation (1560). In 1811, Robert Moffat, the Deputy Controller of the Port of Inverkeithing, built Moffat Cottage. The structure is one storey in front and two storeys in the rear. Moffat's son, also named Robert (1795-1883), was enthralled by Rev. Ebenezer Brown's stories of overseas missions and inspired by them he later became a renowned missionary in Africa. He was the first person to translate the Bible into an African language (Setswana). Rev. Moffat persuaded Dr. David Livingstone (1813-1873), who would become the famous explorer and missionary, to direct his attention to Africa instead of China. Later Dr. Livingstone married Rev. Moffat's daughter, Mary. Whether or not Dr. Livingstone ever spent time at Moffat Cottage is a subject of debate. Aside from a residence, Moffat Cottage has served as a meeting place for the town council as well as a surgeon's office. This photo shows Moffat Cottage in the background and to the right, the war memorial. (Photo courtesy of ILHS.)

These two images from the 1860s show Inverkeithing's distinctive tolbooth located on Townhall Street. Tolbooths were multipurpose buildings. They were the location of the burgh's weights and measures, the jail, and the meeting place for the town council. In 1742, the deacons of the town's five guilds (hammermen, weavers, bakers, tailors, and shoemakers) were admitted to the council. Inverkeithing had a tolbooth as early as 1550. Part of the present four stage tower was constructed in 1754-1755 while the three storey block was built in 1769-1770. The lower stages of the tower date to 1550 or earlier. The tower has the burgh's coat of arms with the ship on the right panel and St. Peter on the left panel. This arrangement is the reverse of the usual depiction. The A listed tolbooth is one of Scotland's oldest existing tolbooths. Aside from their civic functions, tolbooths were important because they were an obvious symbol of municipal authority as well as a source of town pride. In describing the Inverkeithing townhouse, the Royal Commission of the Ancient and Historical Monuments of Scotland commented, *This building is a very fine achievement for a small burgh and it is possibly the most distinguished building in Inverkeithing.* (Photos courtesy of ILHS).

This old postcard photograph shows the tolbooth and the mercat cross. The buildings directly behind the mercat cross did not exist during medieval times and are on an island that blocks High Street and the market place from the tolbooth. This situation would not have been permitted during the times that the market place was an essential component of the town's economy. The tolbooth bell was removed because it was unsafe and is now on display at the civic centre. The bell was made in 1667 by Johannes Burgerhuys of Holland and was gifted to the community by Captain James Bennet and Johan Dickson, town officials. Inside the tolbooth, many interesting artefacts were on display. In the courtroom, stood the old oak charter chest. It contained many historic documents including those by William the Lion and Robert III. In the council chambers, are circular-shaped chairs that date from 1783. There is a steel standard ell measure of 1500 vintage. Over the fireplace were two halberds one with a metal studded shaft and head of exquisite design. To the left of the halberds, was the town drum. Particularly in the 17th century, the drum was an important feature of everday life. The drummer would signal the populace the time to start the day (4 a.m.) and the time to retire in the evening (7 p.m.).

A mercat cross is a market cross located in Scottish burghs (usually royal burghs) where trade and commerce were important aspects of economic life. Later they became the site of community events such as announcements, proclamations, and executions. Inverkeithing's A listed mercat cross is a magnificent structure that soars almost 15 feet in height. Two Scots, James Drummond and J. W. Small, who wrote books about mercat crosses agreed that this was the most beautiful one. Early historians believed that the cross dated from circa 1398, the time of the Duke of Rothesay, the son of Robert III and Annabella, and his marriage to Mary, daughter of the Earl of Douglas. That the royal arms and the Douglas coat of arms adorn the cross lends some credibility to this theory. More recent historians favour an early 16th century date for the monument. Even so, Inverkeithing's market cross still ranks among the oldest of Scotland's 126 existing mercat crosses. In 1688, John Boyd, seeking admission to the guild, carved the unicorn finial as a test piece.

The mercat cross has had three locations. Originally it was situated at the extreme north of High Street. In 1799, it was moved in front of the tolbooth. In 1974, the mercat cross was transferred to a location at the end of Bank Street close to the Thomsoun House to the north and next to the Providence House to the south.

Thomsoun House, an A listed building, is located at 2-4 Bank Street. It was originally a two storey main block structure, but a third storey was added creating a lean-to roof known locally as "toofall". The house is dated to 1617 since the hearth bears that date. An interesting feature of this harled and pantiled building is a three stage corbelled stair tower in the southwest corner. Over the moulded doorway on either side are the initials *I. T.* and *B. T.* and a merchant's mark and an inscription. The initials stand for John Thomsoun, a burgess, and his wife, Bessie Thomsoun. The inscription is taken from Psalm 137 of the Bible and reads as follows: *Except. The Lord. Build. The House. They Labor. In Vain. That Build It.* A window lintel has an inscription in Latin. Thomsoun House was remodeled in 1965. Some of its previous owners were quite illustrious including the Earl of Rosebery (who served as the town's provost from 1704-1720), shipowner Charles Grieg, the father of Admiral Samuel Grieg, and Rev. Ebenezer Brown, the minister of St. John's Church.

King Street, the site of the East Port formerly known as Mill Port, is another of Inverkeithing's major roads. King Street was probably named for Robert III. At the King Street Bridge over the Keithing Burn, there were once two mills. The first one was of 13th century vintage and was situated at the northwest corner of the bridge. A later mill was built at the northeast corner of the bridge and stood five storeys high, but is now demolished. The major interest on the street centres on the Rosebery House at 9 King Street. This dwelling, which predates 1582, is the oldest surviving residence in Inverkeithing. The B listed structure, like the Thomsoun House, has a lean-to shape called "toofall". The house has three storeys in the front and two storeys in the rear and is a L plan townhouse with crow-stepped gables. The house underwent extensive modifications in the seventeenth and eighteenth centuries. The Earl of Rosebery, who owned the house from 1705 to 1711, added the west wing which he called the New Jamm (right). Rosebery House has had a list of other distinguished owners including the Earl of Dundee, the Earl of Lauderdale, and John Dungas, surgeon. Over the doorway of the summerhouse are carved the date of 1717 and the initials J. D. and B. F. which represents the names of John Dungas and his wife, Beatrice Ferguson. In recent years, the Rosebery House has functioned as a boarding house and as a bed and breakfast.

Prior to the 18th century, doocots were a familiar sight in Fife. Pigeons provided meat and eggs in the winter for the wealthy. Pigeon droppings had multiple uses. It was an excellent fertilizer and was used in the production of gun powder as well as in tanning and cloth dyeing processes. Possession of a doocot signified that the owner was wealthy and influential. In the 19th century, improved farming techniques allowed for the feeding of cattle in the winter and the need for doocots' provision of fresh meat waned. At one time, Inverkeithing had at least five doocots. All of them were built in the 17th century and were of the lectern design. The Rosebery House doocot was a moderately large one with 1,335 nesting holes. It was located to the rear of the house in a former orchard. With the construction of Commercial Road in the late 19th century, the doocot is now closer to the new road than to King Street. The construction of Commercial Road adversely impacted Port Street, formerly the major route from the town centre area to the harbour. As a result, many of the houses that once lined Port Street have been demolished. In 1981, the discoveries of an archaeological excavation uncovered some finds that revealed a hint of Port Street's previous importance. Among the discoveries were medieval pottery and garden soil as well as a 17th century spoon, button, and seal. (Photo courtesy of RCAHMS.)

This substantial stone house was located on Alma Street. Where King Street reaches Keithing Burn, the name changes to Alma Street. The street once was known as Gowkhall and Court Gait, but after the Battle of Alma in 1854 (the first major campaign of the Crimean War) the street was renamed in honour of Lord Raglan (FitzRoy Somerset) who once resided on the street and was a key factor in the victory. He had also been involved in the Battle of Waterloo almost forty years before. Another person associated with the street was James Fraser (1898-1987), who was born there. Fraser was a department supervisor at Caldwell's Paper Mill for 43 years and served on the town council for 27 years, including six years as the provost. When the residents of 7 Alma Street were digging in their back garden in 1964, they uncovered a merchant ship's cannon which dates from circa 1780-1810. The cannon was refurbished by Babcock Engineering Services of Rosyth and is now located in front of the Inverkeithing Civic Centre near the friary.

Inverkeithing was blessed with a beautiful, sheltered, and natural harbour. This painting of Inverkeithing Bay projects a feeling of tranquility in an idyllic setting. An author writing in 1857 described Inverkeithing Bay as beautiful as the Bay of Naples although smaller! Industrial development in the latter part of the 19th and in the 20th century altered the scene somewhat. These industries provided many people with employment and were essential to the economic health of the burgh. Benefiting from an excellent location between Edinburgh and the rest of Fife and other towns northward, Inverkeithing was one of Scotland's leading seaports from the 12th century to the 15th century and during the 1327-1331 period, it ranked as the seventh leading Scottish port in terms of custom receipts. Inverkeithing merchants were active on the Continent as late as the 15th century although by 1500 Inverkeithing's foreign trade was insignificant. During the reign of George III (1760-1820), Royal Navy ships were docked at Inverkeithing Harbour during the winter. In the late 18th century and in the 19th century the burgh, bolstered by coal exports from nearby mines, experienced a resurgence in trade. As traffic increased and ship sizes got larger, Inverkeithing's relatively shallow harbour presented a problem. Efforts were made to deepen it, but this improvement was not sufficient or timely enough to keep the trade from moving to larger ports with their deeper harbours and more modern facilities.

Located where the Keithing Burn flows into Inverkeithing Bay, the Caldwell Paper Company was Inverkeithing's largest employer during the 20th century with a peak workforce of 750. In 1892, Gordon Caldwell and others purchased the Inverkeithing Paper Pulp Company and after that "Caldwell" was part of the firm's name. The mill suffered a devastating fire in 1913 (opposite) with the building as well as its contents destroyed. The mill was rebuilt of brick and was operating again by 1914. The design of the new mill was admired by papermakers from the Continent and the United States of America. Caldwell was the Scottish pioneer in the production of grease-proof paper, but due to financial difficulties was sold in 1928 to Inveresk, a company which owned several paper mills. For the next 75 years, the economic fortunes of Caldwell would wax and wane. Caldwell mothballed one of its smaller paper machines and laid off 70 workers in 2000 in an attempt to improve its financial status. Finally, in August of 2003 it shut its doors and the remaining 170 workers lost their jobs. The circa 1930 photograph (left) shows the interior of the mill. The ladies are neat and well-groomed and are in the process of sorting and packaging paper.

NVERKEITHING · PAPERMILL · BURNED 24 MAY 1913

39

This picture shows Inverkeithing Bay, the Caldwell Paper Mill in the centre, on the right, Ward's Shipbreaking Yard, and to the extreme right, Cruicks Quarry.

In the late 19th century, one of Inverkeithing's prime industries was shipbuilding. In the 20th century, shipbreaking proved to be a more profitable enterprise. The Thomas Ward Company opened a shipbreaking yard at Inverkeithing in 1921 and over the next 60 years many ships of different designs were dismantled for their scrap value. One of the most famous ships that ended its journey at Inverkeithing was the *Olympic*. Unlike her sister ship, the *Titanic*, the *Olympic* had a long and distinguished career (1911 to 1935). During the First World War, she served as a troopship and earned the nickname, 'Old Reliable'. For a short time she was the largest ocean liner in the world. Her superstructure was dismantled at Jarrow and her hull was scrapped at Inverkeithing. The photograph shows the *Formidable* at Inverkeithing. She was an aircraft carrier that served in the Royal Navy during the Second World War. Just before the *Formidable* was to be launched a terrible accident occurred. A wooden cradle supporting the ship gave way and the aircraft carrier slid down the launchway killing one and injuring several. As a result of this event, the *Formidable* was referred as *The Ship That Launched Itself*. During the war she saw extensive action in the European, North African, and Pacific theatres and survived several kamikaze attacks although she was hit twice. Alas, this proud ship was determined to be too damaged to repair and in 1949 she was placed in reserve then scrapped in 1953.

In the vicinity of Inverkeithing, quarrying has been a major industry for over 300 years with several quarries in the area operating at various times. The quarrymen in the photograph worked at one of Inverkeithing's quarries. Limestone and sandstone have been quarried, but the most prominent stone extracted has been whinstone. Whinstone is any hard dark rock and is named for the ringing noise a hammer makes when it strikes it. At Inverkeithing the whinstone is a quartz dolerite. Stones from the local quarries were used in the building of the Forth Bridge piers, London roads, the Forth & Clyde Canal, Liverpool Docks, Leith Docks, and the Kronstadt (Russia) Harbour fortifications. Cruicks Quarry commenced operations in 1828. Being very close to the Firth of Forth it was easy to ship its products. The quarry has been dormant recently, but the owner plans to resume operations in the future.

Hillend, Inverkeithing.

About a mile and a half to the north east of Inverkeithing is Hillend. In the past, this tiny village of a couple of hundred people served primarily as a linen weaving community and as a horse station. It provided a horse to assist loaded wagons up the steep hill from St. David's Bay to the main road. This photograph shows Hillend's main street. The first building on the left (the one that a man is leaning against) was the post office.

James IV granted the lands of Fordell to James Henderson in 1511. Henderson had served the king as lord advocate and lord chief justice of Scotland. The first castle on the land was built in 1210 by the de Cameras, a Flemish family. There are a few features of the original castle that are visible in the present castle such as the star and half moon motifs in the dining room, a bedroom, and in the garden. The castle, located about two miles northeast of Inverkeithing, was expanded in 1567, but a fire destroyed much of it. The castle was rebuilt circa 1580. Fordell Castle is an A listed four storey tower house. It has a rectangular main block with square towers at the northeast and southeast corners with corbelled turrets. By 1961, the castle was in near ruins when Sir Nicholas Fairburn, the eccentric but talented Member of Parliament, purchased the property. Sir Nicholas was also chairman of Historic Scotland. He restored the castle and its garden with love, knowledge, and style. and demolished the nearby house with a callous disregard for its historical importance! Since his death in 1997, the castle has had several owners who have also renovated the building. The castle was purchased in 2007 for the fifth largest price of a home in Scotland. Famous visitors to Fordell Castle include Mary, Queen of Scots, author Daniel Defoe, and former Prime Minister Margaret Thatcher, who planted a tree on the grounds of the estate.

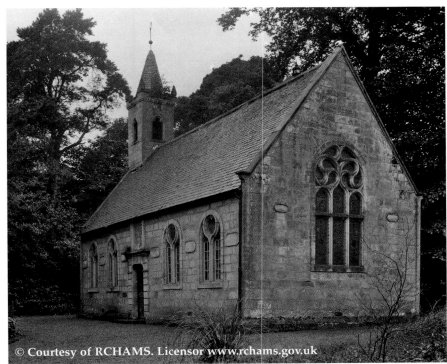

The photograph above shows Fordell Castle Chapel dedicated to St. Theriot. It is not clear who St. Theriot was, and possibly the spelling is a variation of Erat. The A listed chapel was built in 1650 and is about 70 yards from the castle. Described by architects as beautiful and magnificent it is a small edifice measuring 40 feet by 16 feet containing beautiful ironworks from Italy, stained glass and etched windows, and a marble floor (one source says flagstone). It has an altar, pews, and a lectern. The walls are lined with memorials to the Henderson and Fairbairn families. Beneath the chapel is a crypt. Among those buried here are the fifth baron of Fordell and all six of the baronets of Fordell and members of the Fairbairn family including Sir Nicholas Fairbairn. The image to the right is of Fordell House, located close to the castle, which was built in 1721 and became the Hendersons' chief residence although they still maintained the castle for many years. When Sir Nicholas purchased the Fordell estate, Fordell House was rundown and he had it demolished in 1963. The elaborate mansion had 43 rooms.

The Hendersons of Fordell started mining the coal outcroppings near Fordell Castle in 1596 and later dug pits to extract the coal. Originally coal was carried by horse and pannier to Inverkeithing Harbour for export. This method was inefficient because only small amounts of coal could be transported and frequently the roads were impassable because of bad weather. In 1752, Sir Robert Henderson, the fourth baronet of Fordell, constructed a pier at St. David's Harbour, about a mile from Inverkeithing. This then became the destination harbour for Fordell Colliery output. In 1770 a waggonway, which extended about six miles from near Crossgates to St. David's Harbour, was established and it continued until 1833. The waggonway was supplanted by a malleable iron railroad operated by horses and aided by a series of inclined planes. From 1868 to 1946, steel rails powered by steam locomotives were used to transport coal to the port. This railway was the first privately owned railway in Scotland. The image shows William Pit which operated from 1843 to 1950. At the time of its closure, it was the oldest coal mine in Scotland.

To facilitate the mining of coal and its shipment, the Hendersons of Fordell established two small villages. St. David's Bay was a port and had a customs house, a few dwellings and a population of about 140. To make way for the new town of Dalgety Bay, the remnants of this village were demolished in the mid-1960s. The photograph shows the former pier and in the distance is the Forth Bridge. Now it is the location of modern homes and a fashionable marina. North of St. David's Bay was the miners' village of Fordell Square. The village had a population at its peak of 800. For most of the 18th century, Scottish miners were virtual slaves. Late in the 1700s, legislation was passed that gave the miners' more liberties. Sir Robert Henderson implemented the provisions of the new law a year before it was scheduled to take effect. The miners and their families were ecstatic. The tradition of an annual three-day celebration of their new liberties called the Paraud was established and continued for decades. No outsiders were allowed to participate. There were games, bands, dancing, eating, and drinking. One of the traditions was a parade around the town that extended to the nearby Fordell House so that they could pay their respects to the laird and his family.

One of history's greatest engineering accomplishments is the Forth Bridge, located about two miles from Inverkeithing. This photograph taken during its construction looks towards the Fife coast. The massive bridge was completed in 1890 and at the time it was regarded as the eighth wonder of the world. It extends for 1.5 miles connecting Edinburgh with Fife. Its girder spans are 1,710 feet and the towers soar well over 300 feet. At its peak, 4,500 workers were employed building the bridge. In recent years 200 trains daily pass over the bridge. The Forth Bridge was the first structure in the United Kingdom to be built of steel and at the time of its construction it was the longest cantilever bridge in the world. It now ranks second. The Prince of Wales officially opened the bridge by tapping the last rivet, a gold one, in place. The builder of the Eiffel Tower, Gustave Eiffel, was in attendance at the opening ceremony. The Forth Bridge has entered the film culture. The bridge was shown in Alfred Hitchcock's 1935 film, *The 39 Steps*, as well as the 1959 remake of the movie. The bridge is also featured in the 1980 movie, *Bon Voyage, Charlie Brown (And Don't Come Back)*.